Shaking the Sand Out

Shaking the Sand Out

Poems of Motherhood
by

Susan Joy Riback

For Maureen,
In honor of the
art of motherhood +
the joys of
capturing a
moment with
a word.
may you find many
poems + words to
bless your life,
Susan Joy

Poems for Life

Photography and cover design: Phillip Riback
Interior design: Mary Caprio

To my daughters,
Elana and Julia,
my muses

and to Phillip,
my devoted husband.

Table of Contents

More than Mother 65

Acknowledgements

My special thanks to my husband Phillip for all his creative ideas and his enduring patience, to Nadine Stram for her insights and sensitive feedback, to Jan Fleischner-Lewis for her expertise and editing support, and especially to Perie Longo, who inspires me always and generously shares her poetic wisdom, guidance, and humor.

Andrea Bartfield, Jill Crammond-Wickham, Kerstin White, and my loving family, thank you for your encouragement and enthusiasm.

"Whenever we give praise to something,
it becomes more beautiful."
— Perie Longo

Pregnancy
& Early Days

In the beginning months of pregnancy I realized that in the next nine months nothing would be as it used to be. It was through writing poems and journal entries that I learned to appreciate the moods that swung from elation to depression, from the wondrous to the fearful. Writing also helped me hold on during the roller

coaster ride of pregnancy, during the dangerous turns and curves. Years later the poems helped me to remember the details, my cravings for ice cream and cottage cheese as well as the sensuous feelings pregnancy evoked within me.

Everyone told me that a new mom must cherish every moment of those early years because time goes quickly, more quickly than we realize. It was not easy to take time for myself but these small poems tended to my inner thoughts and feelings. Writing in a journal helped me learn to take in precious details, to notice more acutely the dance of mother and child, a baby's soft cheek, or warm fuzzy head. These images are held forever in the arms of a poem to remind me of where the journey began.

Moods of Pregnancy

Carefully we pray
to the creamy white
foods we eat
to baby bones
to blue stars
whose light leaks
through the holes
of our hearts
sprinkling love
all over the planet

In Honor of the Harvest Goddess

Heat wave in my mind
I walk naked in fields
with black cows
staring at my swinging breasts.

I graze all day in this field
a harvest goddess
wheat colored hair
red succulent mouth.

My baby growing inside
stretches under my heart
with the dry grasses
and the shadows' movement
pulsing.

A Found Poem

In 1921 it was advised
not to swing, waltz or sing
for fear of harm
to the occupant of the abdomen
and the doctors warned

let your lodger enjoy
his apartment in peace.

Oh Belly!

Do you love
loving this baby
expanding by the minute?

Do you hold us both
like the arms of the sky
cradle the earth?

Do you hear
the song of my heart
beating yes?

October Birthday

I celebrate your October birthday
with the fertile fall spell
you once had over me,

mother ripe
and waiting

for the leaves in the wind
and the sound of your
first cry.

Magic

Cord wrapped twice
around her neck
at birth

She rose out of the womb
like Houdini,
arms free.

Milk

Milk from the sky
laughing on my head
holy   holy

Milk from my breast
laughing into you
holy   holy

Baby Bliss

Her love accepts all of me
morning breath
messy hair dirty feet.

Slow sleepy warmth
of cradle and lullaby
her fuzzy head
curled into my neck.

"Yes Sir, She's My Baby"

Twenty three inches tall
eleven pounds eleven ounces

Her warm cheek presses to mine
face flushed

We dance slow dances
we rumba

spinning in each other's arms
the greatest of partners!

In Mom and Dad's Bed

Move over sister
I am new born glazed
a witness to china tea

Let me roll in quilted patterns
your hair falls in my face
in my mouth

Move over sister
this morning a dove
broke my hiccups

In a puff of powder
your face folds around me
before fading out

Cheeks

I never want
to forget
this cheek
sweet peach smelling cheek
squirrel cheek chipmunk cheek
cheek cheek
pressed to mine

Summer Postpartum

The house painters outside my window
joke and rattle the roof,
the lawn mower growls.
Julia is asleep,
throbbing thoughts of her are in my milk ducts,
nursing bra overextended in bumper pads of skin.
I am touched by her hiccups all around me.
Everyone is out,
t-tops, bathing suits.
Even with pale legs and hairy knees I wear shorts.
I live inside a cave smelling clean from soap,
body stiff and sore.
I want to eat watermelon,
run and play Frisbee.
I like ice cream better than ice pops,
I like anything on the grill,
last night ate four ears of corn with butter and salt.
I am eager to lay on the grass,
to watch the night sky.
I live every minute inside these walls
in a summerless way.
I will come back to you
moon and sky,
night swallowing me like a hungry bear.
I will be happy to be consumed.

"I Hear the Accident in Her Voice"

Poems Born from My Children's Lips

The precious words that our children speak are gifts, time capsules which hold within them a treasured moment. Once my daughter confused the word "accent" with "accident" saying that she could hear in the foreigner "the accident in her voice." These poems celebrate my children's innocence and special way of looking at the world. After all, they are the astronauts on the moon of our hearts.

Pressing Her Nose Close into the Soft Curve of My Neck

you smell like pennies

Julia's Question

Why are they sitting
in the wind Mommy?
My three year old asks
watching the other family picnic
under the blowing leaves
of a large oak tree
and why Mommy are we sitting
in the other wind?

At Age Three

She tells us
the sky swallowed her
but let her go
like the other baby spirits
like rain.

Prolific

There are a thousand seeds
in every paragraph
of this grapefruit.

Bedtime Ritual

I slowly turn the handle
of Brahms lullaby box
three times
one for good luck

please one more Mommy
I wasn't listening.

Nightmare

My doll has my nightmares
she memorizes them
turning them round
turning them into a beautiful dress.

Words of My Angel Face
"Three in quarters" age

Why do you roll your pants up to your knees,
Julia?
>*to get some fresh air.*

Sitting on my lap, fingering the shape of my
clavicle,
>*Mommy, you have necklace bones*

Preparing dinner Julia comes into the kitchen,
>*can we eat in the diamond room?*

and when Julia eats jelly beans
she lines them up in little families
and eats them one by one
only after telling them
a story

with a happy ending.

My Daughter Learns to Swim

I carry her to the bathroom
 I love you
sleepy warm arms
around my neck
 I'm dreaming a big girl dream
eyes rolling.

She sits on her small potty seat
 I'm dreaming of fishes
 tropical fish
 gold fish...

She rolls into her bed
pillow pink and steamy
swims back to them
swims away.

Name Change

I need a new name
to go with my dress
my pigtails
I am Jessica
not Elana
that's a stupid name

I understand this need
would like to be called Lori
I met a Lori recently
I liked her eyes
her laughter

she can be Susan
I can be Lori
flower dress
pigtails
Jessica

Bazaldo!

Watch this strawberry disappear they whisper
under terryfuzz cape of swimtowel
eyes beaming bright
watch the glow
turn out the lights
we are thrilled, believing
one pulls quarters from the air
the other just stands there smiling

the trick.

Julia on Boys
(age 5-1/2)

Girls are smarter than boys
boys are taller than girls

boys just aren't my life
not my real love
I am not loveable with them

They can't come up to me and say
I love you
and hug me and kiss me

they have to ask

A Rational Heart

At eight and a half my daughter tells me
I do not believe in soul
I do not believe in God

After the Native American unit
in second grade
she believes in Great Spirit
her heart softened with the Mystery

by third grade she feels it is a waste
to believe in something
she cannot prove

I believe in science
I believe in planets
I believe in my body

Even so I say listen and learn
from your head and your heart

my heart is just a big blob that beats
and sends out blood
she explains
growing away

Parent

She rolls her tongue, *can you do this,*
can you, can you, huh?
Sings loudly, look at me, *la la la, look!*
She asks to be liked, *like me like me like me,*
PLEASE.

She is so silly, she says.
but sometimes I forget forget forget
to love her silly enough
being too serious
for a five year old.
I wish   I wish   I wish.

Six in Venice

Seated at a small table,
in L'Osteria di Santa Marina,
eating spaghetti, fresh seafood,

the waiter watches her
dig treasures from the Adriatic
barnacles on mussel shells
chewy pink shellfish
what a good bambina! he says
placing a kiss on the top of her head.

She unfolds the yellow cloth napkin
smoothing linen over her lap
ordering *latte freddo,*
her only Italian words.

On the way home
she finds a white rose left behind
on the bridge Realto,
lets the petals go
one by one into the Grand Canal.

This is the best night of my life, she says.

Seven-Year-Old Love

She gets so excited thinking one day
she will find love and marry
wiggling in her chair she decides
his name will be Bryce.

Oh Bryce, Oh Bryce, Oh Bryce
she chants over her chicken and couscous
like a lovesick movie star
her face grows pale, then paler,
over such love.

Shimmering Chandeliers

Elana asks,
Who will pay for my wedding?
I don't want a wedding
in a run-down hotel
with only forty people
My lecture begins—
love a good man
one who will make you laugh
he should be close to his mother
very intelligent
make you feel safe
it doesn't matter where you get married
as long as friends and family are there
some people elope
don't elope
I will cry at your wedding
you will be a beautiful bride
it's not about fine wines
and shimmering chandeliers—
No, Mom! I don't want a wedding
in a run-down hotel
with only forty people.

Inspired in Italy

Walking arm in arm
through narrow streets in Venice
windows rich in hand-blown glass
precious stones, bird masks,
and postcards,

my eleven-year-old daughter leans in close
one day I will be famous
on Broadway
or a commercial
maybe for Neutrogena face soap?

Somewhere in the distance
the strong voice of a singer
serenades a couple in a gondola
as it glides over the dark waters of Venice

roads turn into water
water turns into roads
here anything is possible.

My Daughter's Back Brace

You might dress it in velvet
put it in a dress shop window
missing legs   a head

it is only one part of you
hips to chest
but oh what a part it is

enclosing your heart
where adolescent dreams
are bound tight within a boy's arms

all that love cased
in that suit of armor
you are your own knight now

you say *hit me*
hit me hard
I feel nothing

What She Remembers of Canada

On the first star she wishes
that the owners of the B&B move to Hawaii
and leave the guest house facing
Mont Tremblant's snow-topped trees
to her and her sister, to cuddle
each morning in a downy king-sized bed

when she will say *you have stinky breath*
and sister says, *you do too—*
moving closer under the warm
sleepy haze
because this is the vacation
she wishes her life was,

horse-drawn sleigh rides over snowy fields.

Lately

things have begun appearing
and disappearing
it is the way of the teenager
taking off on her own wings
one day arriving home in Pat's black
all-star sweatshirt
it smells like Pat—he smells good....I'm keeping it.

and just tonight
trying to even out the few
eyebrows she plucked,
those soft furrowed brows
that once told their own story,

suddenly thinned into a thread
leaving pink tender skin
and open spaces.

Poems of Praise, Guilt, and Gratitude

The challenge of raising small children is learning to live again with the tender ache that accompanies growing up. Writing poems helps me with the complexities of my feelings as I struggle to be the best parent I can be. The most I can do is to accept my feelings of guilt, praise, and gratitude, to embrace them all as one poem does, within its very nature of being a poem.

What You Are to Me

Sleeping moonstone
pancake face
home of clover
fields of flowers
music of my little toe
dance of sun on the sundial
silver flute's sweetly borrowed sounds
tomorrow's window wide open

Shaking the Sand Out

My daughter crab-crawls
digs her nails into wet sand
miles of moonlit grains
in gritty pulsing fingers.
I remember my mother warning
don't bring the sand home.

Later, I find sand in the bed
in the folds of a past relived.
I brush it off
seeing her at sunset
running all over the beach
like a young puppy
taking it all in
taking it everywhere.

Red Berries

Yesterday I yelled at those young girls
for climbing
the tree on the green
outside our house and
throwing red berries
on my daughter's head

when she asked
what's your name?
these tough girls
didn't answer

My daughter
loves their long hair
their climbing rituals
even though it bends the branches
even though I yell at them
for hurting the tree I love.

Beyond Dr. Spock

Ship my daughter is
tossed fragile against forces beyond her
she wants more chocolate
she doesn't want to hear the thunder
of my *No!*
my whisper of *let's talk.*
I shout,
You are driving me crazy!

I am out of Spock's advice
never raise your voice
I put her to bed
soup spilling down her chin
mixed with salty tears.
Between swallows I want to say,
meet you in ten strokes,
keep your eyes on the shore
Go!
but she says, *medicine.*
The opening of her lips
is the sky clearing.

To soothe the icy waves
no matter what the book says
I give her cherry-flavored Tylenol
sweet like chocolate,
the end of the storm.

Daddy's Night

I could be
ringleader
conductor
master of ceremonies

I hear them counting by fives
water isn't running

I could go up
wisk off her undershirt
put her on the potty
wash her hands and face

but I don't.

Satin Heart Pillows

A four-year-old's opium
home away from home.
We take these pillows
wherever we go.

Cradled in our lap
sucking a tiny thumb
she smells the dusty perfume
of the old torn lace.

One day she will feel
the thousand heart pillows
she carries within

closing her eyes
each night
in peace.

Ode to My Five-Year-Old

I sit by the window and wait
for you to step off the kindergarten bus.
Astronaut on the moon of my heart

what island did you discover today?
Wearing pigtails and the color pink
you sing a song
you don't know the words to.

You leave your shoes at the door
like a flag of your country.
Your feet fit in my palm,
flutter like butterflies
over the carpet,

you on a hopscotch course to noon.

First Day of School

Julia carries the bug box outdoors
like a precious urn.
Free! she calls to the cricket
found on the bathroom floor
on this very important morning.
Before boarding the big yellow school bus

she saves one life.

My Pumpkin Girl

How long has it been
since we went to that pumpkin patch?
The first year you said *pumpkin,*
plucking a root from the fallowed field
which, like a rope tied to the core of the earth,
would not release itself.
You went for the pumpkin the earth
intended to give you, not round and perfect
as in a storybook, but unevenly odd
fading yellow, spotted green.
And came to sit with it
between your legs, hoping to grab the stem
and lift its vital orange life.

I tell you now it was a perfect match,
your strong solid legs, hands chubby
and determined
meeting face to face
the plump joy of an October harvest.
You squeezed the immovable pumpkin
so hard we thought it sure to burst open
releasing its wet pulp and seeds into the earth
so you could come again next year
and feast.

Summer Child

To an eight-year-old,
God is a teenage camp counselor
wears a ponytail
cut-off shorts
is in high school
shares her lunch
promises her a pickle
and drives her home.
God is somebody
she gets to hug
whenever she wants
who links her to a larger universe
day after summer day.

The Moon of My Heart

If you look inside my heart
you will see the turkey sandwich
my daughter ate today,
outline of whole wheat crusts
also, leftover peach pits, apple seeds,
and kind words,
the ones saved to plant a tree.

Inside my heart
there is a stream bed,
pine needles spongy underfoot,
natural springs running deep,
sunlight through the trees.

People I love are in my heart
my mother cooking Chicken Miriam,
my father, drawing the details of a bird
he will later paint,
my children and husband
centered in the middle
of the moon of my heart.

The window is wide open,
wind and sun and flower box full
and loneliness, that old ache,
slips out with the cold air.

During the night
a poet leaves notes under my pillow,
wraps her arms tenderly
around everything
loved and cherished.

The Rescue

My daughter and I dive into the opening
of a large green recycling bin
smelling musty attic books
flung anonymously into the abyss
old words soon to be scrapped
into shreds
our legs flailing behind us.

We pull out "Hokysai's Japanese Art"
"Journey to the Far Amazon"
hold each others' limbs
falling far enough in
to rescue ourselves
books still alive.

Growing Up

Her bangs have grown
to cover her eyes
she begs for sleepovers
and when I hug her
she becomes water,
floats away.

I wish
only the roll of the dice
on a game board
moved her forward.

Two spaces.
At the most
six.

I'd always let her win.

Brussels Sprouts

My daughter and I love
the tightly layered leaves
small orbits of spring
uncurling green,
tender warm planets
in our mouths
together eating toward the soft heart.

Samurai

My seven-year-old
likes to bend
her strong legs
wrap
her long arms
tightly

around unsuspecting
schoolmates
raising them high in the air
trophies to her strength.

Though other children
shy away
for fear
of being caught
measured by their lightness

Emelia loves it
loves to be raised above it all
lifts her head
and cheers.

Prickly Pears in Italy

My older daughter
discovers exotic prickly pears,
holds them tenderly
knobby bulbs
brown spots
thorns invisible to the eye
as if each one were a golden egg

until their painful kiss.
Her father removes the prick of each nettle
but cannot
dislodge the stinging.

Small Breasts

My daughter decides pointy is not good
for small breasts
that constantly change their shape.
This day as she looks in the mirror
rounder lines show through
the thin blue cotton, she likes that,
unlike when the nipple tips its hat,
the bra bunches its flowering tissues
into a small pillow filled with stuffing
that has not yet met its corners.

With a tender swollen ache
that might release itself
and become free,
she flattens them with her hand,
but these small dumplings,
inquisitive guests,
win their way again.

Humming

I am thankful for my daughter
humming in the kitchen
without it
my world would crack open
like an empty egg
fragile and thin like my hold
on happiness.

She slips her hand
into mine
and we dance
down the hallway
humming to Natalie Cole singing
love was made for me and you.

Guilt

*You are the world's
worst mother!* she yells

A mother too busy
for her child?

Why
do I believe her?

Disappointing My Daughter

I am not the Other Mother,
the one who gives a party for no reason,
who lets thirty shrieking girls
turn out the lights to play murder,
to dance under a disco ball.

I am not the Other Mother,
who buys the latest fashion at any cost
and volunteers to cook spaghetti
for a fundraiser,
run the after-school bake sale,
choreograph the fifth-grade play.

I am the one daughter knows is Not
but wishes were,
when love disappoints
and The Other Mother shines.

I open my pocketbook heart
dig deeper
for spare change.

Saving Face

This pout you see
after my teenage daughter yells
at me, isn't me.

I am not this woman
glaring viciously.
I am not even sure
I know who becomes me,
my face strangely muscled.

Maybe I am the story whose plot
thickens as it is being told.
This pout you see isn't me
after my teenage daughter yells
but one day, a smiling grandmother
sure she did the right thing.

Her Place

She promises a night of servitude
will serve apple slices
provide blankets and pillows
a small bell to ring
anything to keep her place.

Bird Song

It's morning
I open my eyes and hear
the high pitched chirps
of a five-year-old coming from the bathroom
a ten-year-old singing from the stairs.

Little Guy sings from his white wire cage,
sunlight in his throat.

The children have their own songs.
One is now reading in bed,
the other brings small clay figures to life.

Out of the white wire cage
Little Guy climbs the ladder of our fingers,
sits upon our shoulders,
heads towards the windows' illusion of freedom,

small freedom,
to fly around the kitchen.

My children, my small birds,
rise over me
with powerful wings.

Her Voice

She sings every word
to every song on the radio

like a swollen rain-fed river
she opens her whole body

she sings every word
to every song
growing taller than herself

like trees in the forest
with wild underbrush
she can't stop
rising.

Where She Hides Her Poems

In the pocket of her jeans
run through the wash,
in the puddle of clothes
thrown on the floor,
with the spearmint gum wrappers
falling from her sleeves,

in her hips,
the bony part she loves to feel growing,
in the glossy shine of her lips
when she smiles.

Getting Ready

freshly scented girls
with iridescent love dust
try one outfit on after another

it's Friday evening!

Relocating

One day she wakes up with hips
that swing out like tsunami waves

She stands in front of the mirror
tracing the sharp points
the long curves

as if to map
a new route
to somewhere she doesn't know

Leading Lady

I am the leading lady
who carries the world
on her shoulders and
makes the brights brighter
runs the vacuum over evil.

I am the mother
the one who follows
the bouncing balls
of my children's dreams
the one who stocks chocolate
cookies and milk
the one who treasures baby shoes
book-marks the memories.

I am the recipe for longevity
noodles in peanut sauce
barefoot days
the wilderness of the future.

I am the leading lady
the picnic planner
the one who brings the pie.

Picking Up an Adolescent Daughter from School

She is embarrassed
by the banana
I bring her

One Reason to Hold Tightly

I read in the news
that half of the baby rats
sent into space

floated away
from their mothers.

More than Mother

How do we really get by as mothers? For one, we learn to complain, to express in any way possible our struggles, hopes, and dreams. The other important lesson is to remember the many sides of us, that we are more than just mothers. We need to continue to sing "dirty laundry blues" or lament the loss of the sensual goddess as she moves through us. Perhaps we no longer "gather in the driveway" as our mothers once did, but we need to be a part of a community. We need to invite others to join us, as we attempt to do the most important work of harboring children while they learn to set sail on their own...

Forget-Me-Nots

Parenting you is like growing
forget-me-nots

Clusters of sky-blue blossoms
face sparkling with light
eyeshadow and glitter
lacy spray of hair falling softly

I am the tree standing tall
you enter my shade
cover my roots and spread
knowing well
how to take in sun and rain
while I watch
unmoving

your dance around me
your blue songs.

Home from Camp

Elana pulls a hair
from my chin
a long
single
stubble,
yanks it right out,
so happy to be home.

I become
more beautiful.

Pay the Ransom

Today I feel like a hostage
tied to a kitchen chair

waiting the hours
while the wild rice boils
the teakettle whistles
can't dream sitting upright

this was to be my day
to revolve around the earth
to lose myself in the round
of a high hayloft
to take the wind's path

What price?

Morning Ritual

Children off to school
I put away
Cheerios   raisin bagels   toast

prepare cappuccino filled with
imported Belgian chocolate
wrapped in gold paper

everything life was made for

the sun inside my mouth
the sumptuous suck and melt.

Not Sleeping In

It is the morning that you can sleep in
that the cat comes,
sniffing your left ear
licking your neck
kneading small paws
into your cushioned slumber,

a snowy morning
when the oldest daughter
comes crawling first
between you and your husband,
wisps of hair falling over your face
a dreamslung arm pinning you down.

It is the morning you don't set an alarm
when the second child
trots in on tiptoes
climbing the quilted landmass
of cat, sister, father,
settling against your weakening wall.

When the covers no longer cover,
when an unmindful elbow has no kindness,

the morning you rise
like the snow angels
who leave their sleeping shapes
without remorse.

Seeker

I'm growing an Ushnisha
like the Buddha of the 4th century
a topknot
signifying
superhuman
perfection

I'm gazing
from the altar
of my spiritual aura
hair in tiny curls
sensuous body visible
beneath
transparent robe

Buddha
never claimed to be
anything
but human
when he found
the path
to truth

but I impatient mother
cowlick sticking straight up
six thirty in the morning
grumbling
to wake my daughter

must try
for Nirvana
again

Mothers Gather in the Driveway

On the driveway discussing the delights
of our children, those sweet Chinese apples
cross our tall shadows
towards our watchful eyes.

Beloved names kept under our tongue
words like almond fig clover
we talk of breadfruit

standing on the grasshopper course
they chalked minutes before
they stepped out from behind weatherglass
shouting *Hawkweed!*

We gather and illuminate
draw them back at dusk
fluttering like gypsy moths.

The Weakest Part of Me

Last night in my dream I cried to my husband
I can't go on failing this way...
word problems I can't figure
cross multiplication.

Why does this bother me?
I have children now
I write poetry
I have a fine calculator

but in this particular dream
I am intimidated
by the student next to me
so proud of herself
knowing there is only one
right answer.

Limited by my logic
limping through percentages
unsure how much to tip

I must take the test over.

Work Boots and Other Turn-ons

I've been too long at home
stacking clean dishes
when the man with dark eyes
arrives in a big red truck
ladder on side.

He has tan leather work boots
faded jeans
a grey sweatshirt
that fits like a winter sky
over a meadow,

wild blackbird hands
he says can fix anything.
When I ask, *how long?*
he says, *until you kick me out.*

My heart jumps like a car engine
turning over on a cold morning.
Did I imagine it,
or did he slightly raise his brow,
deepen his gaze up on the silver steps
of the long ladder?

He connects
wires in the ceiling to an earthquake box,
assures me
there will never be an earthquake.

What a morning!
he has the right lines,
he keeps me safe
he takes all day,

I like a man that takes all day.

Goddess Moved through Me

Tonight I danced the dance of the goddess,
the teacher taught figure eights, earth energy,
saying, *open open*
hips becoming beams of arced angles
tipping the earth
every move a devotion of the flesh.

Braver tonight I showed a little belly
between crop-top and leggings
knees slightly bent
pelvis tucked
the coins sewn to my hip-scarf jangled
as the goddess emerged from me,
ancient with her dance of secret desire
waving with the arms of my arms.

Your husband will love that, a friend told me,
as if I could do this at home,
open petals with undulation
turn in twisted shapes of half moons
to the sounds of Raptured Rumi.

She does not know how fleeting
the dance of a housewife is,
as the goddess moved through me and on

to another woman,
one with devouring eyes
and hips.

Dirty Laundry Blues

We've got the dirty-laundry-under-the-bed blues
dirty laundry under the bed blues
the where-did-it-go-how-did-it-get-there
wash-it-all-away blues.

Older child's trail of tried on clothes
little one's hair bands brushes and bows
my husband's long long overdue
'cause his work is never through.

We've got the let's-get-together-never-find-time blues
the out-of-breath-hurry-up-aren't-we-having-fun blues
get-out-of-bed-don't-stop-till-you-drop
achin'-for-peace-of-mind blues.

Neighbors got 'em—they're never at home
best friend got 'em—she's cryin' on the phone
daughter's got 'em—cause she ain't got no clothes
though drawers are full of stuff and won't even close.

Give us a rest, oh blues,
Give us a sign, it's comin' soon
gotta stop folding laundry before dawn
Oh blues, give us a bed to sleep on.

Flexible

Children running
through your house
laughing louder than the wind
knocking over the crystal
running through you
with colored streamers.

Let them.

Circular Breath

As I sit here
breathing slowly in
breathing slowly out

As I sit here
behind a thin veil of self
skin thin and translucent

As I sit here
small hopes pass through
like scents of lilac
first days of an open window

A Chinese screen of woven silk
my soul's shadow moves through

as I sit here
breathing in breathing out
the last yell
that shook the house

As I sit here
with patient flow of streams
in quiet woods

This Poem Is Nothing Like a Baby

Babies in yellow
soft doughy bundles
big sunbursts of smiles
mother cooing and kissing

Now the rocking
of a shadow
the swaddling of a soul
poem growing for a lifetime

is born to the page
and when I tire
I can put down my pen

I'd Take a Pill

I'd take a pill to turn me back into the girl
    who laughed easily
I'd take a pill to untie my feelings from the knot
    inside my stomach
a pill to loosen my grip on the steering wheel
a pill to make me want my husband to kiss me
a pill to make me not worry that my daughter
    will be teased
a pill to make me want to volunteer at school
I'd take a pill to stop me from telling my children
    to drink water
or they will become dehydrated
to eat a healthy snack and not a yodel
to brush their teeth even when they say they did
    but I know they didn't
a pill to let underwear stay where it falls
a pill to make it possible to put up my feet
eat popcorn even if kernels fall between the cushions
a pill to make me mischievous and giddy
I'd take a pill that would let me forget myself
and one to remember myself
a pill that helps me say I need…
a pill that shuts my mouth
a pill that makes me sit on the rug and play
    with my daughters' pink plastic ponies
I'd take a pill to turn my body into an embodied body
a pill to make me sing while I clean, cook
    and make sandwiches

continued

a pill that turns off judgment and releases fear
a pill that babysits
a pill that asks friends, family, and loved ones
    to forgive me
a pill that holds me when I cry
I'd take a pill to quiet the barking dog
    of my mind.

Bus Station Dream

There is a bus
waiting in a diesel fumed stall
your name in big letters
above the driver's seat

look out silver chromed windows
unevenly opened
calculate the distance to a future
when the children are gone

Another life to board
prepare yourself for the long ride
although it will feel like you've never left

No Time to Listen

As a mother
I always answer
to small voices

Inside myself
a lost poem
a lost day
a flood of forgiveness
for who I am

My children
whom I love
embrace
all my promises

As a mother
I always answer
to small voices

wishing
for my own